A Place Like Heaven

An Introduction to the Synod of Dort

Samuel Miller

Log College Press

www.logcollegepress.com

A Place Like Heaven: An Introduction to the Synod of Dort
By Samuel Miller

© 2019 by Log College Press

Log College Press
92 Cotton Wood Dr.
Madison, MS 39110
www.logcollegepress.com

Page and cover design by Clay Meyer
Printed in the USA by Color House Graphics, Grand Rapids, MI

ISBN: 978-1-948102-18-6 (booklet)

ISBN: 978-1-948102-19-3 (ePub)

ISBN: 978-1-948102-20-9 (Mobi)

Foreword

Conservative Presbyterians rightly have a fondness for Old Princeton. Our attention tends to gravitate towards those theological giants Charles Hodge and B.B. Warfield, but these men would not have been who they were if it were not for Samuel Miller (1769-1850). Miller became the second faculty member of Princeton Theological Seminary, alongside Archibald Alexander, appointed to teach ecclesiastical history and church government. His work as an early professor at Princeton laid a foundation of Reformed orthodoxy that remained until the modernist controversies. Miller was a productive preacher and a prolific professor. His extant writings are numerous. In addition to his voluminous correspondence, we also have his works on church polity, describing eldership and defending the antiquity of the Presbyterian structure.[1] Further, he wrote a thorough, multi-volume history of the eighteenth century.[2] This selection is still only a sample of his works, and merely a brief synopsis of his contributions to the American Presbyterian legacy.[3]

Miller's present essay introduced Thomas Scott's work on the Synod of Dort.[4] There is, however, a multi-layered background to this introduction. The Synod of Dort (November 13, 1618 – May 9, 1619) convened to deal with theological controversies within the Dutch Reformed church surrounding the teaching of James Arminius (1560-1609) and his followers, known as the Remonstrants. The Remonstrants submitted a set of five articles, called the Remonstrance, to outline their views. The Synod, composed of international Reformed theologians from around the Continent and a British Delegation, responded with a document addressing each of the five articles in turn, and this document became the confessionally binding Canons of Dort to which Dutch Reformed churches still subscribe and from which

---

1. Samuel Miller, *An Essay on the Office of the Ruling Elder* (1831); Miller, *The Warrant, Nature, and Duties of the Office of the Ruling Elder* (1835); Miller, *Presbyterianism: The Truly Primitive and Apostolical Constitution* (1840); Miller, *Letters on Unitarianism* (1821); Miller, *Letters on the Eternal Sonship of Christ* (1823); Miller, *Letters on Clerical Manners and Habits* (1827).

2. Samuel Miller, *A Brief Retrospect of the Eighteenth Century* (1803, 1805).

3. For an extended biography, see Samuel Miller [Jr.], *The Life of Samuel Miller, D.D., LL.D.* (1869). Many of Miller's works can be found on his author page on the Log College Press website (www.logcollegepress.com/authors-mr#/samuel-miller-17691850).

4. Thomas Scott, *The Articles of the Synod of Dort* (1818; repr., Philadelphia: Presbyterian Board of Publication, 1841).

we gather the famous (but reductionistic) five points of Calvinism. Thomas Scott (1747-1821), an Anglican, wrote his volume to introduce and explain this Synod and its conclusions in order to speak Reformed theology into an Anglican context that was still very much colored by the ascendancy of proto-Anglo-Catholicism that had gained ground with the Restoration and secured preeminence at least within the reign of George I (1660-1727). Scott believed that Reformed theology was not only misunderstood by its opponents, but also misrepresented. He sought to clarify and restate the tenets of the Reformed faith as they are expressed in the Canons of Dort, which honed in on the issues surrounding predestination, and to demonstrate that these doctrines regarding God's sovereignty are not in conflict with the practical conduct of gospel ministry. Scott's lengthy treatise provides a thorough introduction to the Synod of Dort and a translation of its Canons into English.

Miller's essay introduced American audiences to the Synod of Dort, about which Joseph Hall said there was "no place upon earth so like heaven." Miller first commended the Synod of Dort in comparison to the Westminster Assembly, an event more familiar to his American colleagues, then provided background on James Arminius, painting him as a subverting influence of Reformed orthodoxy. After detailing the Arminian controversy that erupted in the Netherlands and provoked the Synod, he described the events of the Synod and some of its more notable contributors, outlining how these debates affected England and the American colonies, specifically on the issue of religious toleration. Miller explained why Thomas Scott wrote this volume, and he joined in the refutation of the idea that Calvinism makes God the author of sin. Instead, it affirms God's grace in salvation.

Miller's introduction to Scott's work still helpfully presents the issues and figures at the Synod of Dort. It also reveals that American Presbyterians have long treasured our Reformed heritage, even joining with Christians of other polities, like Thomas Scott, in the proclamation of God's saving grace. In days like our own when the ritualism of Anglo-Catholicism has lured even some conservative Presbyterians, Miller's essay reminds us that the stalwarts of Anglicanism that we should appropriate are those who were vigorously Reformed. Further, we as Presbyterians should care deeply about our theological history, and Miller's essay will inspire us all to read more about it.

Dr. Harrison Perkins
London

A Place Like Heaven

The convocation and proceedings of the Synod of Dort may be considered as among the most interesting events of the seventeenth century. The Westminster Assembly of Divines was, indeed, more immediately interesting to British and American Presbyterians; and the works of that celebrated Assembly, as monuments of judgment, taste, and sound theology, have certainly never been equalled by those of any other uninspired ecclesiastical body that ever convened.[1] Yet the Synod of Dort had, undoubtedly, a species of importance peculiar to itself, and altogether pre-eminent. It was not merely a meeting of the select divines of a single nation, but a convention of the Calvinistic world, to bear testimony against a rising and obtrusive error; to settle a question in which all the Reformed Churches of Europe had an immediate and deep interest. The question was, whether the opinions of Arminius, which were then agitating so many minds, could be reconciled with the Confession of the Belgic Churches?[2]

The opinions denominated Arminian had been substantially taught long before Arminius appeared. The doctrine of Cassian, of Marseilles, in the fifth century, commonly styled Semi-Pelagianism, was almost exactly the same system.[3] Bolsec, too, in Geneva, about the year 1552, according to some, had also taught very much the same doctrine, though justly regarded as infamous on account of his shameful moral delinquencies.[4] And about fifteen or twenty years before Arminius arose, Corvinus, in Holland, had appeared as the advocate of opinions of similar import.[5] But having less talent than Arminius, and being less countenanced by eminent men, his error made little noise, and was suffered quietly to sink into insignificance, until a stronger and more popular man arose to give it new consequence, and a new impulse.

---

1. The Westminster Assembly first convened on July 1, 1643 and last officially met in the Spring of 1653.
2. The Belgic Confession was written chiefly by Dutch pastor Guido de Brès in 1561, and revised by various Synods before and at the Synod of Dort.
3. John Cassian (c. 360-c. 435) was a Christian monk and mystical writer.
4. Jérôme-Hermès Bolsec (died c. 1584) was a French Carmelite theologian who converted to Protestantism but engaged in controversy with John Calvin.
5. Johannes Arnoldi Corvinus (c. 1582-1650) was a Dutch Remonstrant minister.

James Arminius, or Harmensen, was born at Oudwater, in south Holland, in the year 1560. His father died when he was an infant; and he was indebted to the charity of several benevolent individuals for the whole of his education. At one time he was employed as a servant at a public inn, and in this situation was so much noticed for his activity, intelligence, wit and obliging deportment, that numbers became interested in his being enabled to pursue the cultivation of his mind.[6] Accordingly, by one of his patrons, he was placed, for a time, in the University of Utrecht; on his decease, by another, in the University of Marburg, in Hesse; and finally, by a third, in that of Leyden. In 1582, in the twenty-second year of his age, the magistrates of Amsterdam had received such impressions of his promising talents, and of his diligent application to study, that they sent him, at the public expense, to Geneva, which was then considered as the great center of theological instruction for the Reformed Churches. In that far-famed institution Theodore Beza then presided, with equal honor to himself, and acceptance to the students.[7] Here Arminius, as before, manifested much intellectual activity and ardor of inquiry; but indulging a spirit of self-sufficiency and insubordination, in opposing some of the philosophical opinions held and taught by the leading professors at Geneva, and delivering private lectures to turn away the minds of the students from the instructions of their teachers, he became a kind of malcontent, and was constrained to withdraw from that Institution. This circumstance somewhat impaired that confidence in his prudence which his patrons had before reposed. Still they were willing to overlook it.

After travelling eight or ten months in Italy, he returned for a short time to Geneva, and soon afterwards to Holland, where he met with no small acceptance in his profession. Such was his popularity, that, in 1588, he was elected one of the ministers of Amsterdam, and entered on a pastoral charge in that city, with every prospect of honor, comfort, and usefulness. But his restless, innovating spirit soon began, in his new situation, again to disclose itself. Not long after his

---

6. [S.M.] Life of Wallaeus, one of the members of the Synod of Dort. [Johannes Walaeus, "Vita Antonii Walaei," in Antonius Walaeus, *Opera Omnia Tomus Primus* (Lugduni Batavorum: Adrian Wyngaerden, 1647), sig. A*4r-******4r. The biographic details of Arminius appear on sig. ***4v-***5r.]

7. Theodore Beza (1519-1605) was a French Protestant Reformer and theologian.

settlement, the doctrine of Beza concerning Predestination was publicly opposed by some ministers of Delft, in a tract which they printed on this subject. When this publication appeared, Martin Lydius, professor of Divinity at Franequar, having a high opinion of the learning and talents of Arminius, judged him to be the most proper person he was acquainted with to answer it; and, accordingly, urged him to undertake the task.[8] Arminius, in compliance with this request from his venerable friend, undertook to refute the heretical work; but during the examination of it, and while balancing the reasoning on both sides, he went over to the opinion which he had been employed to refute; and even carried it further than the ministers of Delft had done. This change of opinion, which took place about the year 1591, and which he was not long in causing to be understood, soon excited public attention. About the same time, in a course of public lectures, delivered in his own pulpit, on the Epistle to the Romans, he still further disclosed his erroneous views. He was soon accused of departing from the Belgic Confession, and many of his brethren began to look upon him and his opinions with deep apprehension. Such, however, were the vigilance and firmness manifested by the other members of his Classis, that they so far curbed and counteracted him as to prevent the agitation of the controversy, which it seems to have been his intention to excite. Arminius, however, though deterred, at that early period, from public and open controversy, exerted himself in a more private way, with considerable effect. With some divines, whose friendship he had before conciliated, his talents, his learning, his smooth address, and his insinuating eloquence were successful in winning them to his opinions. The celebrated Uytenbogart and Borrius were among the number of his early converts and followers.[9] He also took unwearied pains to gain over to his cause some of the leading laymen of the country, and so on enlisted several of them in his cause.

In the year 1602, when the illustrious Francis Junius, an eminent Reformer, and no less eminent as a Professor of Divinity in the University of Leyden, was removed by death, to the great grief of the Belgic churches, Uytenbogart, who

---

8. Martin Lydius (1539-1601) was a Dutch theologian.

9. Johannes (or Jan) Uytenbogaert (1557-1644) was a Dutch Protestant leader of the Remonstrant party. Adrianus Borrius (1565-1630) was President of the University of Leiden. Miller's spellings of names and places have been retained in the text throughout.

was just mentioned as a particular friend and partisan of Arminius, proposed, and, with great zeal, recommended him to the Curators of the University, as a candidate for the vacant Professorship.[10] The leading Belgic ministers, hearing of this recommendation, and deeply apprehensive of the consequences of electing such a man to so important a station, besought both Uytenbogart and the Curators of the University to desist from all attempts to place in such an office one who was the object of so much suspicion. But these entreaties were disregarded. The recommendation of him was prosecuted with undiminished zeal, and the Curators at length elected and formally called him to the vacant chair.

The call being laid, as usual, before the Classis of Amsterdam, that body declined to put it into his hands. They supposed that he was more likely to prove mischievous in the office to which he was called than in his pastoral charge, where he was more immediately under the supervision and restraint of his brethren in the ministry. But, at length, at the repeated and earnest entreaties of Uytenbogart, of the Curators, and of Arminius himself, he was permitted to accept the call, and was regularly dismissed from the Classis to enter on his new office. This dismission, however, was granted upon the express condition, that he should hold a conference with Gomarus, one of the theological Professors in the same University with that to which he was called;[11] and should remove from himself all suspicion of heterodoxy by a full and candid declaration of his opinions in regard to the leading doctrines of the Gospel; and, moreover, the Classis exacted from him a solemn promise, that, if it should be found that he held any opinions different from the Belgic Confession, he would refrain from disseminating them. This conference was held in the presence of the Curators of the University, and the Deputies of the Synod, in the course of which Arminius solemnly disavowed Pelagian opinions;[12] declared his full belief in all that Augustine had written against those opinions; and promised in the most explicit manner that he would

---

10. Francis Junius the Elder (1545-1602) was one of the most celebrated Protestant divines of his day.
11. Franciscus Gomarus (1563-1641) was a Dutch Protestant pastor and theologian.
12. Pelagius (c. AD 360-418), opposed by Augustine of Hippo, was a British theologian who denied the doctrine of original sin and affirmed an unbiblical doctrine of human freedom.

teach nothing contrary to the received doctrines of the Church. Upon these declarations and promises he was placed in the Professorship.

On first entering upon his Professorship he seemed to take much pains to remove from himself all suspicion of heterodoxy, by publicly maintaining theses in favor of the received doctrines – doctrines which he afterwards zealously contradicted. And that he did this contrary to his own conviction at the time, was made abundantly evident afterwards by some of his own zealous friends. But after he had been in his new office a year or two, it was discovered that it was his constant practice to deliver one set of opinions in his professorial chair, and a very different set by means of private confidential manuscripts circulated among his pupils.[13] He was also accustomed, while he publicly recommended the characters and opinions of the most illustrious Reformed divines, artfully to insinuate such things as were adapted, indirectly, to bring them into discredit, and to weaken the arguments usually brought for their support. He also frequently intimated to his pupils, that he had many objections to the doctrines usually deemed orthodox, which he intended to make known at a suitable time. It was observed, too, that some pastors who were known to be on terms of great intimacy with him, were often giving intimations in private that they had adopted the new opinions, and not a few of his pupils began to manifest symptoms of being infected with the same errors.

The churches of Holland observing these and other things of a similar kind, became deeply apprehensive of the consequences; they, therefore, enjoined upon the Deputies, to whom the supervision of the church was more especially committed, to inquire into the matter, and to take the earliest and most decisive measures to prevent the apprehended evil from taking deeper root. In consequence of this injunction, the Deputies of the churches of North and South Holland waited on Arminius, informed him of what they had heard, and urged him, in a friendly manner, if he had doubts or difficulties respecting any of

---

13. [S.M.] This fact, so dishonorable to the integrity of Arminius, is so well attested by various Dutch writers of undoubted credit, that it cannot be reasonably called in question. [Modern historiography still supports the fact that in the midst of controversy, Arminius was "less than forthcoming about his views." Richard A. Muller, "Arminius and the Reformed Tradition," *Westminster Theological Journal* 70 (2008): 47, 22-23.]

the received doctrines of the Belgic churches, either to make known his mind in a frank and candid manner to his brethren in private; or to refer the whole affair, officially, to the consideration and decision of a Synod.

To this address of the Deputies Arminius replied, that he had never given any just cause for the reports of which they had heard; but that he did not think proper to enter into any conference with them, as the Deputies of the churches; that if, however, they chose, as private ministers, to enter into a conversation with him on the points in question, he was ready to comply with their wishes; *provided* they would engage, on their part, that, if they found anything erroneous in his opinions, they would not divulge it to the Synod which they represented! The Deputies, considering this proposal as unfair, as unworthy of a man of integrity, and as likely to lead to no useful result, very properly declined accepting it, and retired without doing anything further.

In this posture of affairs, several of the magistrates of Leyden urged Arminius to hold a conference with his colleagues in the University, before the Classis, respecting those doctrines to which he had objections, that the extent of his objections might be known. But this he declined. In the same manner he treated one proposal after another, for private explanation; for calling a national Synod to consider the matter; or for any method whatever of bringing the affair to a regular ecclesiastical decision. Now a Classis, then a Synod, and at other times secular men attempted to move in the case; but Arminius was never ready, and always had insurmountable objections to every method proposed for explanation or adjustment. It was evident that he wished to gain time; to put off any decisive action in the case, until he should have such an opportunity of influencing the minds of the leading secular men of the country as eventually to prepare them to take side with himself. Thus he went on evading, postponing, concealing, shrinking from every inquiry, and endeavoring secretly to throw every possible degree of odium on the orthodox doctrines, hoping that, by suitable management, their advocates both in the church and among the civil rulers might be gradually diminished, so as to give him a good chance of a majority in any Synod which might be eventually called.

This is a painful narrative. It betrays a want of candor and integrity on the part of a man otherwise respectable; which it affords no gratification even to an adversary to record. It may be truly said, however, to be the stereotyped history of the commencement of every heresy which has arisen in the Christian church. When heresy rises in an evangelical body, it is never frank and open. It always begins by skulking, and assuming a disguise. Its advocates, when together, boast of great improvements, and congratulate one another on having gone greatly beyond the "old dead orthodoxy," and on having left behind many of its antiquated errors: but when taxed with deviations from the received faith, they complain of the unreasonableness of their accusers, as they "differ from it *only in words.*" This has been the standing course of errorists ever since the apostolic age. They are almost never honest and candid as a party, until they gain strength enough to be sure of some degree of popularity. Thus it was with Arius[14] in the fourth century, with Pelagius in the fifth, with Arminius and his companions in the seventeenth, with Amyraut[15] and his associates in France soon afterwards, and with the Unitarians in Massachusetts, toward the close of the eighteenth and the beginning of the nineteenth centuries. They denied their real tenets, evaded examination or inquiry, declaimed against their accusers as merciless bigots and heresy-hunters, and strove as long as they could to appear to agree with the most orthodox of their neighbors; until the time came when, partly from inability any longer to cover up their sentiments, and partly because they felt strong enough to come out, they at length avowed their real opinions. Arminius, in regard to talents, to learning, to eloquence, and to general exemplariness of moral deportment, is undoubtedly worthy of high praise: but if there be truth in history, his character as to integrity, candor, and fidelity to his official pledges and professions, is covered with stains which can never by any ingenuity be effaced.

At length, after various attempts to bring Arminius to an avowal of his real opinions had failed, he was summoned by the States General, in 1609, to a conference at the Hague. He went, attended by several of his friends, and met Gomarus, accompanied with a corresponding number of orthodox divines. Here

14. Arius (AD 256-336) was a theologian who denied the divinity of Jesus Christ.
15. Moses Amyraut (1596-1691) was a French theologian at Saumur who tried to synthesize Arminian ideas with Reformed theology by revising the traditional understanding of God's decrees. He argued that God first decreed to save humanity by faith through Christ's satisfaction, which meant the cross was truly universal both in its value and intent, and then God subsequently elected some to faith because he foresaw that human inability prevented people from bringing themselves to faith.

again the sinister designs and artful management of Arminius and his companions were manifested, but overruled; and he was constrained, to a considerable extent, to explain and defend himself. But before this conference was terminated, the agitation of his mind seems to have preyed upon his bodily health. He was first taken apparently in a small degree unwell, and excused himself for a few days, to the States General; but at length grew worse; was greatly agitated in mind; and expired on the 19th day of October, 1609, in the forty-ninth year of his age. His mind, in his last illness, seems to have been by no means composed. "He was sometimes heard," says Bertius, his warm friend and panegyrist, "He was sometimes heard, in the course of his last illness, to groan and sigh, and to cry out, 'Woe is me, my mother, that thou hast borne me a man of strife, and a man of contention to the whole earth. I have lent to no man on usury, nor have men lent to me on usury; yet every one doth curse me!'"[16] Attempts have been made to show that Arminius did, in fact, differ very little from the received doctrines of the Belgic churches; nay, that he, on the whole, coincided with sublapsarian Calvinists; and of course, was most unjustly accused of embracing the heresy since called by his name. It is evident that Dr. Mosheim, himself an Arminian, was not of this opinion.[17] He plainly thought, that the friends of the Belgic Confession had much more reason to apprehend hostility on the part of Arminius and his followers, to the essential principles of their creed, than their published language would seem to intimate. And the Rev. Dr. Murdock, the latest and best translator of Mosheim, has delivered the following opinion, which will probably commend itself to the judgment of all well-informed and impartial readers:[18]

"It is a common opinion that the early Arminians, who flourished before the Synod of Dort, were much purer and more sound than the later ones, who lived and taught after that council; and that Arminius himself only rejected Calvin's doctrine of absolute decrees, and its necessary consequences, while, in everything else, he agreed with the Reformer; but that his disciples, and

---

16. Petrus Bertius (1565-1629) was a Flemish theologian, scholar, and cartographer.
17. Johann Lorenz von Mosheim (1693-1755) was a German Lutheran church historian.
18. James Murdock (1776-1856) was known for his translation of Mosheim's *Institutes of Ecclesiastical History*.

especially Episcopius, boldly passed the limits which their master had wisely established, and went over to the camp of the Pelagians and Socinians.[19] But it appears to me very clear, that Arminius himself revolved in his own mind, and taught to his disciples, that form of religion which his followers afterwards professed; and that the latter, especially Episcopius, only perfected what their master taught them, and casting off fear, explained it more clearly. I have as a witness, besides others of less authority, Arminius himself, who, in his will, drawn up a little before his death, explicitly declares that his aim was to bring all sects of Christians, with the exception of the Papists, into one community and brotherhood. The opinion that Arminius himself was very nearly orthodox, and not an Arminian, in the common acceptation of the term, has been recently advocated by Professor Stuart, of Andover, in an article expressly on the Creed of Arminius, in the *Biblical Repository*, No. II., Andover, 1831, see pp. 293 and 301.[20] To such a conclusion the learned Professor is led, principally, by an artful and imposing statement made by Arminius to the magistrates of Holland, in the year 1608, one year before his death, on which Mr. Stuart puts the most favorable construction the words will bear. But from a careful comparison of this declaration of Arminius, with the original five articles of the Arminian creed (which were drawn up almost in the very words of Arminius, so early as the year 1610, and exhibited by the Remonstrants in the conference, at the Hague, in 1611; and were afterwards, together with a full explanation and vindication of each article, laid before the Synod of Dort, in 1617, changing, however, the dubitation of the fifth article into a positive denial of the saints' perseverance), it will, I think, appear manifest, that Arminius himself actually differed from the orthodox of that day, on all the five points; and that he agreed substantially with the Remonstrants on all those doctrines for which they were condemned in the Synod of Dort. And that such was the fact, appears to have been assumed without hesitation by the principal writers of that and the following age, both

---

19. Simon Episcopius (1583-1643) was a Dutch theologian of the Remonstrant party.
20. Moses Stuart, "Creed of Arminius, with a Sketch of His Life and Times," *Biblical Repository* 1, no 2 (1831): 226-308. Moses B. Stuart (1780-1852) was an American Congregationalist theologian.

Remonstrants and Contra-remonstrants."[21]

It was fondly hoped by many that when Arminius died, the controversy to which his speculation had given rise, would have died and been buried with him. But this, unhappily, by no means, proved to be the case. It soon appeared that a number of Belgic divines of no small name had embraced his sentiments, and could by no means be persuaded to desist from propagating them; and in 1610 they were organized into a body, or formal confederacy; and in this capacity presented to the States General an address which they styled a Remonstrance, from which the whole party afterwards obtained the name of Remonstrants. The particular object of this paper was to solicit the favor of the government, and to secure protection against the ecclesiastical censures to which they felt themselves exposed. This step amounted to a kind of schism, and greatly distressed the Belgic churches. Another event soon occurred which excited deeper and still more painful apprehension among the friends of orthodoxy. When the Curators of the University came to fill the professorial chair which had been rendered vacant by the death of Arminius, the Deputies of the Churches earnestly besought them to select a man free from all suspicion of heterodoxy, as one of the best means of restoring peace to the University and the Church. But to no purpose. The Remonstrants had, by some means, so prepossessed the minds of the Curators, that Conrad Vorstius, a minister and professor at Steinfurt, in Germany, a man suspected of something much worse than even Arminianism, was selected to fill the office, and Uytenbogart, one of the most able and zealous of the Arminian party, was appointed to go to Steinfurt, to solicit his dismission and removal to Leyden.[22] The orthodox ministers and churches protested against this choice. They compared it to "driving a nail into an inflamed and painful ulcer;" and earnestly besought the States General not to permit a step so directly calculated still further to disturb and corrupt the churches. Vorstius had, a short time before, published a book *De Natura et Attributis Dei*, and had also edited, with some

---

21. [S.M.] Murdock's Mosheim III, 508, 509. [It is not apparent which edition of Murdock's work Miller was using, but the quote can be found in a later edition: Johann Lorenz Mosheim, *Mosheim's Institutes of Ecclesiastical History, Ancient and Modern*, translated by James Murdock, 3 vol. (New York: Robert Carter, 1858), 3:445.]

22. Conrad Vorstius (1569-1622) was a German-Dutch theologian of the Remonstrant party.

alterations, a book published by Socinus the younger, on the Scriptures, from both which it appeared that he leaned to Socinian opinions.[23] Notwithstanding this, however, the Remonstrants were bent on his election, and it was with the utmost difficulty that their plan for placing him in the vacant chair was defeated. In short, their conduct in the case of Vorstius alone was quite sufficient to show, that the apprehensions of the orthodox concerning the corrupt character of their opinions, were by no means excessive or unjust.

James I, king of England, having read the book of Vorstius, a book concerning the nature and attributes of God, and conceiving it to be replete with radical error, addressed a letter to the States General, exhorting them "not to admit such a man into the important office of teacher of theology; and, further, commanded his ambassador at the Hague to use his utmost influence to prevent the introduction into such a Professorship, of a man, as he expressed it – rendered infamous by so many and great errors, and who ought to be banished from their territories, rather than loaded with public honors." "In short," said the king, "since God has been pleased to dignify me with the title of 'Defender of the Faith,' if Vorstius is kept any longer, we shall be obliged not only to separate from those heretical churches, but also to consult all the other Reformed churches, in order to know which is the best way of extirpating and sending back to hell those cursed heresies which have recently sprung up; we shall be forced to forbid the young people of our kingdom to frequent such an infected University as that of Leyden."

By these and various other sources of influence, the Remonstrants were scarcely prevented from putting Vorstius into the vacant Professorship. Still, though disappointed, they were not disheartened, or diminished in number. On the contrary, the election, soon afterwards, of Episcopius, a leading man of their party, to a Professorship in the University of Leyden, seemed to give them new strength and new hopes. It became also more and more evident that some men of no small influence in the civil government of the country, had become friendly to the Remonstrants, and strongly disposed to pursue a course which should secure at least impunity to them as a party. Hence the repeated manifestation of

---

23. Fausto Paolo Sozzini, also known as Faustus Socinus (1539-1604), was an Italian theologian who founded the school of Socinianism.

unwillingness on the part of the States General to promote the convening of a National Synod, or the adoption of any other plan for bringing the Remonstrants to discipline. It was evidently the favorable object of the Remonstrants and their friends, both in church and state, to do nothing; to secure the toleration of the growing errors; and to allow the Remonstrants as good a standing as the orthodox in the national church. Accordingly, when anxious efforts were made, in 1611, and again in 1618, to bring the affairs of the Church to an adjustment and pacification, the friends of truth were baffled and disappointed. Every effort to bring on a crisis, or, in any form, to call the Remonstrants to an account, was resisted and evaded; and the state of things was, every day, becoming more distressing and alarming. Confusion, and even persecution ensued. Some of the orthodox pastors were suspended, and others driven from their charges, because they could not conscientiously receive those who avowed Arminian opinions into the communion of the Church.

In this situation of things, when the very pillars of society seemed to be shaken; when the ruling powers of the State were seen to be more and more favorable to the erroneous party; and when everything portended the approach of a tremendous crisis – it pleased God to employ an instrument for promoting the advancement of his cause who by no means loved that cause, and who yet was placed in circumstances which at once prompted and enabled him to favor it. James I, king of England, a man of very small mind, and of still less moral or religious principle, having been born and bred in a Calvinistic community, and coming to the throne of England when the leading clergy of that part of his dominions, as well as of the North, were almost unanimously Calvinistic, he fell in with the fashionable creed, and was disposed, as his manner was, in everything, officiously to exert his royal power in its favor. He, therefore, in the year 1617, addressed a friendly, but admonitory letter to the States General, in which he earnestly recommended the calling a national synod, to vindicate the genuine doctrines of the Reformation, and to restore tranquility to the agitated Belgic churches. About the same time, Maurice, the prince of Orange, and the Head of the United Provinces, took the same ground, and urged the same thing.[24] When

---

24. Maurice of Orange (1567-1625) was the leader of nearly all the Dutch territories from 1585 until his death.

the Arminian party perceived that the popular current was beginning to run in this direction, and that there was some prospect of a national synod being called, they were filled with uneasiness, and strove by all the means in their power to prevent it. But their evasive and intriguing arts were now in vain: and although they began to manifest a spirit more like revolt and sedition than before, yet now the state of the public mind was such, that their violence only served to show the greater necessity of some efficient measure for meeting and subduing their turbulence.

At length a decree was issued by the States General in 1618, ordering that a National Synod should convene in the following November, at Dort, a considerable city of South Holland. The method prescribed for the convocation of this synod, was, that a provincial synod should meet in each of the provinces, from which six persons should be delegated to attend the General Synod. And, in most cases, the plan adopted was to appoint four ministers, and two ruling elders from each of the provincial synods, together with at least one Professor from each of the universities.

It had been originally intended that this Synod should be formed of delegates from the Belgic churches only; but at the pointed request of James I, king of England, seconded, at his suggestion, by Maurice, prince of Orange, it was determined to invite eminent divines from foreign churches to sit and vote in the Synod. Accordingly letters were addressed to the king of Great Britain; to the deputies of the Reformed Churches of France; to the Electors of the Palatinate and Brandenburgh; to the Landgrave of Hesse; to the four Protestant Cantons of Switzerland, viz. Zurich, Berne, Basle, and Schaffhausen; and to the Republics of Geneva, Bremen, and Embden, whom they entreated to delegate some of their most pious, learned, and prudent theologians, who, in conjunction with the deputies of the Belgic churches, should labor to compose the differences, and decide the controversies which had arisen in those churches.

The Reformed churches of France, in compliance with the request made to them, appointed Andrew Rivet and Peter du Moulin, as their delegates to attend this Synod; but just as they were about to set out for Dort, in pursuance of their appointment, the king of France issued an edict, forbidding their attendance.[25]

---

25. André Rivet (1572-1651) and Pierre Du Moulin (1568-1658) were French Huguenot theologians.

In consequence of this interdict, the churches of France were not represented in the Synod.

It would be wrong to omit stating, that, before the Synod came together, a day of solemn prayer and fasting was appointed, to deprecate the wrath of God, and to implore his gracious presence and blessing on the approaching Assembly. This day was appointed by the States General, and observed with great solemnity.

The Synod convened, agreeably to the call of the States General, in the city of Dort, on the 13th day of November, A. D. 1618. It consisted of thirty-nine Pastors and eighteen Ruling Elders delegated from the Belgic churches, together with five Professors from the Universities of Holland; and also of Delegates from all the foreign Reformed churches which had been invited to send them, excepting those of France, before spoken of. The delegates from the foreign Reformed churches on the Continent, all of whom were Presbyterian, were nineteen. The delegates from Great Britain were five, viz: George Carleton, bishop of Llandaff; Joseph Hall, Dean of Worcester, and afterwards Bishop, successively, of Exeter and Norwich; John Davenant, Professor of Divinity in the University of Cambridge, and afterwards Bishop of Salisbury; Samuel Ward, Archdeacon of Taunton, and Theological Professor in the University of Cambridge; and Walter Balcanequal, of Scotland, representing the Established Church of North Britain.[26] The Synod thus constituted, consisted, in all, of eighty-six members. No Arminians, it would appear, were elected members of the Synod, excepting three from the Province of Utrecht; and of these only one was admitted to a seat.

It is perfectly evident from the foregoing statement, that the leading divines, and the governing policy of the Church of England, at the date of this Synod, were very far from sanctioning the spirit which has since risen in that establishment, and which has manifested itself, for a number of years past, among many of that denomination of Christians in the United States. Here we see a prelatical bishop and three other dignitaries of the Church of England, two of whom

---

26. George Carleton (1559-1628), Joseph Hall (1574-1656), John Davenant (1572-1641), and Samuel Ward (1572-1643) were English Anglican divines. Ward was one of the translators of the King James Bible and a non-attending member of the Westminster Assembly. Walter Balcanquhall (1586-1645) was a Scottish divine who supported the English monarchs and the Laudian party.

were afterwards bishops, sitting in a solemn ecclesiastical body, and, for months together, deliberating, praying, and preaching with an assembly, all of whom but themselves, were Presbyterians. This was a practical recognition, of the strongest kind, of the Presbyterian Church, as a true Church of Christ; and demonstrated that the great and learned and good men who directed the counsels of the Church of England at that time, never thought of denying, either in word or act, her just claim to this character. Some highchurchmen, indeed, of modern times, either ignorant of facts, or so prejudiced as to be totally blind to the lights of history, have alleged that the States General pointedly requested the king of England to send delegates to this Synod; and that he, unwilling to reject their solicitation, was over persuaded to depart, on one occasion, from the principles which ordinarily governed him and his Church. This statement is altogether incorrect. The solicitation was all the other way. The king of England, though he had nothing, strictly speaking, to do with the business, seemed fond of meddling with it; interposed from time to time in a way in which no other than a weak, officious, pedantic, and arrogant man would have thought of doing; and pressed the States General to adopt a plan which would open the way for the admission of delegates from his Church to the Synod.

And to his wishes and policy in this matter his leading divines acceded. It would have been difficult to select men of more respectable character for talents, learning, piety, and ecclesiastical influence than those who were nominated and commissioned to take their seats in that Synod. They deliberated for months with Presbyterians; preached in Presbyterian pulpits; united in Presbyterian devotions; recognized Presbyterian churches as sister churches, and their ministers as brethren in office and in hope. O how different the language of many prelatists of later times – many of them, it must be confessed, indeed, pigmies in talents, learning, and piety, when compared with the giants who acted their parts on the occasion of which we speak!

When Bishop Hall took leave of the Synod, from which he was obliged to retire on account of ill health, he declared, "There was no place upon earth so like heaven as the Synod of Dort, and where he should be more willing to dwell" (Brandt's *History*, Session 62);[27] and the following extract from a Sermon which he delivered in Latin, before that venerable Synod, contains a direct and unequivocal acknowledgment of the Church of Holland as a true Church of Christ. It was delivered November 29, 1618, and founded on Ecclesiastes 7:16. "His serene majesty, our King James, in his excellent letter, admonishes the States General, and in his instructions to us hath expressly commanded us to urge this with our whole might, to inculcate this one thing, that you all continue to adhere to the common faith, and the Confession of your own and the other churches; which if you do, O happy Holland! O chaste Spouse of Christ! O prosperous republic! This, your afflicted Church, tossed with the billows of differing opinions, will yet reach the harbor, and safely smile at all the storms excited by her cruel adversaries. That this may at length be obtained, let us seek for the things which make for peace. We are brethren; let us also be colleagues! What have we to do with the infamous titles of party names? We are Christians; let us also be of the same mind. We are one body; let us also be unanimous. By the tremendous name of the Omnipotent God; by the pious and loving bosom of our common mother; by our own souls; by the holy bowels of Jesus Christ, our Savior, my brethren, seek peace, pursue peace." (See the whole in the *Acta Synodi Nat. Dord*, 38.)[28]

But this excellent prelate went further. A little more than twenty years after his mission to Holland, and when he had been made Bishop of Exeter, and advanced to the diocese of Norwich, he published his Irenicum (or Peacemaker), in which we find the following passage: "Blessed be God, there is no difference, in any essential point, between the Church of England and her sister Reformed Churches. We unite in every article of Christian doctrine, without the least variation, as the full and absolute agreement between their public Confessions and ours testifies. The only difference between us consists in our mode of constituting the external ministry; and even with respect to this point we are

---

27. Dutch minister and historian Gerard Brandt (1626-1685) wrote a history of the Reformation (1668-1674); the quotation can be found in the English translation of his work: Gerard Brandt, *The History of the Reformation and Other Ecclesiastical Transactions In and About the Low-Countries*, 4 vol. (London: John Nicks, 1722), 3:204.

28. The records for session 16 on November 29, 1618 are recorded in: *Acta Synodi Nationalis…Dordrechti* (Lugduni Batavorum: Isaaci Elzeviri, 1620), 39-46.

of one mind, because we all profess to believe that it is not an essential of the Church (although in the opinion of many it is a matter of importance to her well-being), and we all retain a respectful and friendly opinion of each other, not seeing any reason why so small a disagreement should so produce any alienation of affection among us."[29] And after proposing some common principles, on which they might draw more closely together, he adds, "But if a difference of opinion, with regard to these points of external order, *must* continue, why may we not be of one heart, and of one mind? or why should this disagreement break the bonds of good brotherhood?" (*Irenicum*, Sect. 6).

The same practical concession was made by the Rev. Bishop Davenant, another of the delegates to the Synod of Dort, from the Church of England. After his return from that Synod, and after his advancement to the bishopric of Salisbury, he published a work in which he urged, with much earnestness and force, a fraternal union among all the Reformed Churches. A plan which involved an explicit acknowledgment that the Reformed Churches, most of which were Presbyterian, were true Churches of Christ, and which, indeed, contained in its very title a declaration that these churches "did not differ from the Church of England in any fundamental article of Christian faith." The title of the work is as follows: *Ad Fraternam Communionem inter Evangelioas Ecclesias restaurandam Adhortatio; in eo fundata, quod non dissentiant in ullo fundamentali Catholicae fidei articulo* (*Cantab.* 1640).[30]

But to return to the Synod of Dort. It was opened on the 18th of November, 1618. John Bogerman, one of the deputies from Friesland, was chosen moderator, or president; and Jacobus Rolandus, one of the ministers of Amsterdam, and Herman Faukelius, minister of Middleburg, his assessors, or assistants.[31] The two secretaries were Sebastian Dammannus; minister of Zutphen, and Festus

---

29. Joseph Hall, *The Peace-Maker, Laying Forth the Right Way of Peace in Matter of Religion* (London, 1647), 50-51.

30. "An Exhortation Concerning the Brotherly Communion that Must Be Restored between Evangelical Churches: In Which it Has Been Established that There Is No Disagreement in Any Fundamental Article of the Catholic Faith." Special thanks to Dr. Harrison Perkins for the English translation of Davenant's title.

31. Johannes Bogerman (1576-1637) was a Frisian Protestant divine. Jacobus Rolandus (1562-1632) and Herman Faukelius (1560-1625) were Dutch Protestant divines.

Hommius, minister of Leyden.

Each of the members of the Synod, before proceeding to business, took the following solemn oath, or engagement: "I promise before God, in whom I believe, and whom I worship, as being present in this place, and as being the Searcher of all hearts, that during the course of the proceedings of this Synod, which will examine and decide, not only the five points, and all the differences resulting from them, but also any other doctrine, I will use no human writing, but only the word of God, which is an infallible rule of faith. And during all these discussions, I will only aim at the glory of God, the peace of the Church, and especially the preservation of the purity of doctrine. So help me, my Savior, Jesus Christ! I beseech him to assist me by his Holy Spirit!"

It was some time before the delegates of the Remonstrants, or Arminian party, made their appearance. At the twenty-second session of the Synod, Episcopius, and his twelve colleagues, who had been summoned for this purpose, presented themselves to make their explanation and defense. In undertaking this task, they manifested the same disposition to delay, to elude inquiry, and to throw obstacles in the way of every plan of proceeding that was proposed. Episcopius was their chief speaker; and with great art and address did he manage their cause. He insisted on being permitted to begin with a refutation of the Calvinistic doctrines, especially that of reprobation, hoping that, by placing his objections to this doctrine in front of all the rest, he might excite such prejudice against the other articles of the system, as to secure the popular voice in his favor. The Synod, however, very properly, reminded him, that they had not convened for the purpose of trying the Confession of Faith of the Belgic Churches, which had been long established and well known; but that, as the Remonstrants were accused of departing from the reformed faith, they were bound *first to justify themselves*, by giving Scriptural proof in support of their opinions.

To this plan of procedure they would by no means submit. It disconcerted their whole scheme; but the Synod firmly refused to adopt any other plan. This refusal, of course, shut the Remonstrants out from taking any part in the deliberations of the body. Day after day were they reasoned with, and urged to submit to a course of proceeding ecclesiastically regular, and adapted to their situation, but without success. They were, therefore, compelled to withdraw. Upon their departure, the Synod proceeded without them.

The language of the President (Bogerman) in dismissing the Remonstrants was rough, and adapted to give pain. He pointedly charged them with fraudulent proceedings, with disingenuous acts, with falsehood, etc. For this language, however, he alone was responsible. It had not been dictated or authorized by the Synod. And a number of the members, we are assured, heard it with regret, and expressed their disapprobation of it (Hales's Works, III. 123).[32] And yet, while this language was severe, and, for an ecclesiastical assembly unseemly; was it not substantially, according to truth?

The Synod does not appear to have accomplished its work by referring different portions of it to different committees; but the plan adopted was to request the divines from each country represented in the Synod to consult together, and bring in their separate opinions or judgments in regard to the main points in controversy. So that the sentence, or opinion of the Dutch divines, of the English divines, of the Genevese divines, etc., were separately obtained, and distinctly recorded in the proceedings of the Synod. This method of conducting the business was probably less favorable to dispassionate and perfectly calm proceedings than if committees had matured in private every part of the work.

The Synod examined the Arminian tenets; condemned them as unscriptural, pestilential errors; and pronounced those who held and published them to be enemies of the faith of the Belgic churches, and corrupters of the true religion. They also deposed the Arminian ministers; excluded them and their followers from the communion of the church; suppressed their religious assemblies; and by the aid of the civil government, which confirmed all their acts, sent a number of the clergy of that party, and of those who adhered to them, into banishment. From a large part of their disabilities, however, the Remonstrants, after the lapse of a few years, were relieved.

It is probable that all impartial persons, who make up an opinion with that light, and those habits of thinking with regard to religious liberty which we now possess, will judge that some of these proceedings were by far too harsh

---

32. John Hales, *The Works of the Ever Memorable Mr. John Hales of Eaton*, 3 vol. (Glasgow: Robert & Andrew Foulis, 1765). Hales (1584-1656) was an English Anglican theologian who was sent by the British ambassador to the Netherlands to attend the Synod of Dort as an observer.

and violent. To suppress the religious assemblies of the Remonstrants, by secular authority, and to banish their leaders from their country, were measures which we cannot, at this day, contemplate but with deep regret, as inconsistent with those rights of conscience, which we must regard as indefeasible. But when we consider that those rights were really understood by no branch of the Christian Church at that day; when we recollect that in the Church of England, during the reign of the same James I, who sent representatives to this Synod, more than twenty persons were put to death for their religion, at least two of whom were burnt alive, viz. Bartholomew Legate, at Smithfield, by the direct influence of Dr. King, Bishop of London;[33] and Edward Wightman, at Litchfield, by the equally direct influence of Bishop Neill, of Litchfield and Coventry;[34] and that many hundreds were banished their country; and when we recollect that even the pious Puritans, who migrated from their own country to America, that they might enjoy religious liberty, persecuted, in their turn, even unto death for the sake of religion; and especially when we remember the disingenuous, provoking, unworthy course by which the Remonstrants had divided and agitated the Belgic churches for a number of years; and also the highly unbecoming language which they employed even before the Synod;[35] when all these things are considered, it is presumed no impartial man will wonder, though he may weep, at some of the proceedings of that far-famed and venerable Synod. After all, however, there can be no doubt that a large part of the violence popularly ascribed to that Synod, existed only in the imaginations, the complaints, and the books of the Remonstrants; who were not, of course, impartial judges. The learning, piety, and venerable character of the great and good men who composed it, ought to be

---

33. Bartholomew Legate (c. 1575-1612) was a Socinian who was the last person in London to be burned alive for heresy. John King (d. 1621) was an English Anglican churchman.

34. Edward Wightman (c. 1580-1612) was an English radical Anabaptist and Socinian who was the last person in England to be burned alive for heresy. Richard Neile (1562-1640) was an English Anglican churchman.

35. [S.M.] See Hales's Letters from the Synod of Dort, Vol. III, p. 69, 80, 101, etc. [These letters are found in Johan Lorenz Mosheim (ed.), *Johannes Halesii Historia Concili Dordraceni*, 3 vol. (Hamburg, 1724). Some of the letters are also included in an English edition: "Mr. Hales Letters from the Synod of Dort," in *Golden Remains of the Ever Memorable Mr. John Hales* (London, 1659).]

considered as an ample guaranty of the decorum of their proceedings. But, more than this: if the Synod had not been entirely decent in its mode of conducting business, can we imagine that Bishop Hall, one of the English delegates, a man remarkable for the piety, benevolence, and amiableness of his character, would have said, "There was no place upon earth which he regarded as so like heaven as the Synod of Dort, or in which he should be more glad to remain"? Surely the testimony of such a man is more worthy of confidence than the statements of men who were smarting under the discipline of the Synod.

I have said that the Synod condemned the Remonstrants. In this they were *unanimous*. The Canons of the Synod, which contain their decision with regard to the five Arminian articles, and which are presented in this volume,[36] were adopted without a dissenting voice. We are not, however, to suppose from this fact, that all the members of the Synod were entirely of one mind in regard to all the points embraced in those articles. This was by no means the case. There was much warm discussion during the transactions of the Synod. Some members of the body, such as Gomarus, and others, were advocates of the most high-toned Supralapsarian Calvinism; while another portion of the members were not disposed to go further than the sublapsarian hypothesis; and though all agreed in condemning the Remonstrants, yet a very small number of the delegates appear to have occupied ground not very different from that which we commonly called Baxterian.[37] The Canons, however, were such as they could all unite in. The praise which Dr. Scott bestows on the Formulary of Faith drawn up by the Synod, as a wise, moderate, well digested, and well expressed exhibition of theological principles, is well merited. It is worthy of high commendation. It must be confessed, indeed, that, as a monument of ecclesiastical wisdom, taste, sound learning, judgment, and singular comprehensiveness, the results of the Westminster Assembly, a few years afterwards, not a little exceed those of Dort; but the latter stand next in order, on the scale of Synodical labors. Among all

---

36. Miller refers here to Thomas Scott's book, which he was introducing.

37. Richard Baxter (1615-1691) was an English clergyman who held a version of hypothetical universalism concerning the extent of Christ's satisfaction and stirred controversy in his own time by denying the imputation of Christ's active obedience and reintroducing works into justification.

the uninspired theological compositions of the seventeenth century, many of the best judges are of the opinion that the "Confession of Faith" and "Catechisms" framed by the Westminster Assembly, hold the very highest place. The writer of this page is free to confess that he has never seen any human document of that age, or, indeed, of any other, public or private, which, in his estimation, is quite equal to them for the purpose which they were destined to answer.

The Synod of Dort continued to sit from the 13th of November, A.D. 1618, to the 29th of May, 1619. It held, in all, one hundred and eighty sittings; and was conducted entirely at the expense of the States General.

Dr. Mosheim speaks with more than his usual candor when he treats of the heat and violence which broke out, on various occasions, in Holland, in the course of the Arminian controversy; and especially of the political animosity which unfortunately became intimately connected with that theological and ecclesiastical dispute, and which led to the beheading of Oldenbarneveldt, and to the banishment of Grotius, Hoogerbeets, and others.[38] The truth is, in a number of cases, the political aspect of the subject became the prominent one. The consequence was, that many men became implicated in it who laid no claim to piety; hence the frequency with which the affair had the appearance of a contest among politicians rather than Christians. Still it is believed that even these secular struggles have been magnified for the sake of blackening the anti-Arminian body, who happened to be connected with the strongest political party.

In the Church of Holland, the majority against the Remonstrants, and in favor of orthodoxy, was very large. Judging from the number of ministers reckoned in the established church, and among the Remonstrants, the latter did not constitute more than a thirtieth part of the population. And the proportion remains pretty much the same still: for although since that time the number is greatly increased, among the ministers of the Dutch churches, of those who embrace Pelagian and Semi-Pelagian sentiments; yet many who agree with the Remonstrants in doctrinal opinions, and even some who go much further in

---

38. Johan van Oldenbarnevelt (1547-1619) was a Dutch statesman. Hugo Grotius (1583-1645) was a Dutch jurist and Biblical commentator. Rombout Hogerbeets (1561-1625) was a Dutch jurist and statesman.

heresy than they, do not take their name, or unite with their societies, as the Remonstrants labor under civil disabilities, which multitudes who substantially agree with them in sentiment, do not choose to incur by openly joining their ranks.

After the death of the Prince of Orange, A.D. 1625, the Remonstrants began to be treated more mildly. The ministers were recalled from their banishment, and restored to their functions and churches; and from that period to the present, have been tolerated in the United Provinces, and more lately since the change of government, in the kingdom of Holland. Indeed, it is melancholy to say, that, for a number of years past, in the kingdom of Holland, Pelagian and Unitarian sentiments have obtained such currency in the church of that country, that the only difficulty has been for the friends of truth to obtain permission to preach, unobstructed, the pure Gospel.

Although the many and great evils which always result from the civil establishment of religion, may not have been so strongly exemplified in the Church of Holland, as in some other countries, yet through the whole of the controversy now in question, as well as on various occasions since, we have seen that this unhallowed connection, however coveted by worldly minded ecclesiastics, in all cases stands in the way of the simple and pure dispensation of the Gospel, and never fails to be a curse rather than a blessing. And this, we may confidently say, has been, substantially, the judgment of the best men in all ages in which any just sentiments on this subject have prevailed or been cherished at all. Mr. Gibbon, if I mistake not, has somewhere observed, with a sarcastic sneer, that he is sorry to say, that the earliest and most zealous advocates of religious liberty, have ever been *laymen*, and not ministers of religion.[39] However well-informed that learned infidel may have been on other subjects, he is here under a mistake which, however, may be easily accounted for. The character of his mind, and the habits of his life led him to a much more intimate acquaintance with the writings of laymen and worldly minded ecclesiastics, than with the works of evangelical and orthodox ministers. No wonder, then, that he was ignorant of some testimony on this subject, which, had he been acquainted with it, would

---

39. Edward Gibbon (1737-1794) was an English historian and author *The History of the Decline and Fall of the Roman Empire* (1776-1788).

have led to a different judgment. When the Priscillianists, in the fourth century, were persecuted and delivered over to the secular arm to be punished with death, who lamented and opposed the cruel oppression which they endured?[40] Martin, Bishop of Tours, an eminently pious man, with a number of others of like spirit, mourned over the treatment which they received, remonstrated against it, and pronounced it a *novum et inauditum nefas* ["a new and unprecedented wrong"].[41] And in regard to the writers on the subject of religious liberty in the seventeenth century, to whom there was probably a special reference in the remark which is now combatted, the simplest statement of facts will show that the earliest, and most thoroughgoing advocates of religious liberty, at that period, were all ecclesiastical men; and all of that class with which Mr. Gibbon would be neither likely nor disposed to have much acquaintance.

In 1614, the Rev. Leonard Busher, a zealous Brownist, or ultra-Independent minister, presented to King James I and his Parliament, "Religious Peace, or a Plea for Liberty of Conscience."[42] The leading object of this treatise is to show, that the true way to make a nation happy is, "to give liberty to all to serve God according as they are persuaded is most agreeable to his word; to speak, write, print peaceably and without molestation in behalf of their several tenets and ways of worship." In a few years afterwards, the Rev. John Robinson, a divine of the Church of England, who had been bred at the University of Cambridge, and fled from persecution in his native country to Holland, where he cast in his lot with the Independents, published two works, one entitled "A Justification of Separation from the Church of England;" and another in explanation and defense of the first, entitled "A Just and Necessarie Apologie," etc.[43] In these works he contended with no small force, both of learning and argument, that Christ's kingdom is not of this world; that it is entirely spiritual, and He its spiritual King; and that civil magistrates have no right to interfere, in any wise, or in any

---

40. Priscillian (died c. AD 385) was a Roman Christian bishop from the Iberian Peninsula who led a movement which embraced a Gnostic-Manichaean heresy.
41. Martin of Tours (AD 316/336-397) was an Hungarian-French Christian bishop who opposed the violent persecution of the Priscillianists.
42. Leonard Busher (c. 1573-c. 1651) was an English Brownist author.
43. John Robinson (1576-1625) was an English Separatist who served as the "Pastor of the Pilgrims" while they resided in the Netherlands.

case, with liberty of conscience. In 1644, the celebrated Roger Williams, a native of England; a graduate of the University of Oxford; who had received orders in the Established Church of England; who came to New England in 1630, and there cast in his lot with the Independents; and ultimately becoming a Baptist, withdrew from Massachusetts to Rhode Island, where he became the pastor of the first Baptist church in the American Colonies, and established a separate government, published a work under the following title – "The Bloody Tenet of Persecution for the cause of Conscience," in which he plead for liberty of conscience on the broadest and most liberal principles.[44] In short, he carried the doctrine to the utmost length, and maintained that the civil magistrate has no right to enforce any of the precepts contained in the first table of the Decalogue. And, what is still more to the honor of Roger Williams, as he was, in a sort, the civil ruler, as well as the spiritual guide, of the colony of Rhode Island, it deserves to be recorded that he was the first Governor who ever practically acknowledged that complete liberty of conscience was the birthright of man, and who really and consistently yielded it to those who widely differed from him, when he had the full power to withhold it.

In 1649, the Rev. Dr. John Owen, educated in the University of Oxford, and afterwards Vice-Chancellor of that University, universally known to have been an eminent Independent minister, and one of the greatest theologians of his age, published a work on "Toleration," which does honor to his memory, and deserves to be ranked among the best publications on that subject.[45] He does not, indeed, in his theory, go quite so far as Roger Williams; yet he explicitly states, and by a variety of arguments maintains, that "the civil magistrate has no right to meddle with the religion of any person whose conduct is not injurious to society, and destructive of its peace and order." And it ought to be stated, to the honor of this great and good man, that he acted on the principles which he had avowed, when his own party was triumphant, and he had it in his power to oppress. It is also further worthy of notice, that, some years after the publication of this work, when the Puritans in New England were, most inconsistently, persecuting the Baptists

---

44. Roger Williams (1603-1683) was an English-American Puritan minister and founder of the colony of Rhode Island.
45. John Owen (1616-1683) was an English Independent Puritan theologian.

and Quakers, Dr. Owen, at the head of a body of Nonconformist ministers in London, sent an address to them, remonstrating against their conduct, and entreating them to cease from their persecuting measures, which, accordingly, they soon did. The language of this address is striking and to the point. Among other things it is said, "We make it our hearty request, that you will trust God with his truth and ways, so far as to suspend all rigorous proceedings in corporeal restraints or punishments on persons that dissent from you, and practice the principles of their dissent, without danger or disturbance to the civil peace."

Perhaps the learned reader will be apt to ask, why the name of Bishop Jeremy Taylor has not a place assigned in this list of advocates for religious liberty.[46] The reason for not giving him a conspicuous place in this honored catalogue, will appear from the following statement. In the year 1647, that great and eloquent man, who has been strongly styled "the Shakespeare of the English pulpit," published his "Liberty of Prophesying," in which a great deal of important truth on this subject is communicated, with a power for which the author was distinguished in all his works. The writer, however, argues chiefly from considerations which do not hold a legitimate, and certainly not a primary place among the controlling arguments on this subject. For example, he reasons in favor of religious liberty, from the difficulty of expounding the Scriptures so as to arrive at any certain conclusion on some points; from the incompetency of Popes, Councils, or the Church at large, to determine articles of faith; from the innocence of error, where there is real piety; and from the antiquity and plausibility of various sentiments and practices generally held to be erroneous. It is more on such grounds as these that he rests his defense of toleration, than on the inherent and essential rights of men, and the authority of the word of God. Such an advocate can scarcely be recognized as pleading for the same principles with Williams, Owen, and his other clerical contemporaries in the same nominal field.

But there is another, and still more serious objection to our assigning to Jeremy Taylor an honorable place in the list of early and able advocates of religious liberty. When he wrote his work on the "Liberty of Prophesying," he and his church were under the frown of government. He was, in fact, pleading

---

46. Jeremy Taylor (1613-1667) was an English Anglican churchman and author.

for toleration for himself and for Episcopacy. When Charles II was restored to the throne; when Taylor came forth from retirement and oppression; and when he was raised to the Episcopate, he consented to become a member of the privy council of that faithless and profligate monarch, from which so many persecuting edicts against the nonconformists issued, to the disgrace of their author. And even if it be doubted whether he ever took any active part in the persecuting edicts of that monarch, as a member of his council, yet it is notorious and unquestionable, that in his diocese in Ireland, he was chargeable with much and severe persecution. If he ever entertained correct sentiments in respect to the rights of conscience, he forgot or disregarded them all when he rose to power, and was enabled to persecute. (See Orme's *Life of Owen*, p. 101; and the *History of the Presbyterian Church in Ireland*, by James Seaton Reid, D. D. M. R. S. A. p. 344, etc.)[47]

While justice is done to the ministers of the gospel above mentioned, I have no desire to derogate, in the least degree, from the credit due to Milton, and Locke, of the same century, whom it is the fashion to eulogize, as the great pioneers in pleading for religious liberty.[48] There is no doubt that both these illustrious laymen wrote nobly in defense of the cause in question; and that both ought to be held in grateful remembrance for their noble services; yet it is surely wrong to ascribe to them, meritorious as they were, all the credit of originating a doctrine which had been held, and publicly defended many years, before either of them had published or written a line on the subject.

The National Synod of Holland has never met since the adjournment of the Synod of Dort, in 1619. By the fiftieth article of the Rules of Government which that Synod adopted, it was prescribed that a general Synod should meet every three years, but not without the approbation of the civil government. This article, however, has never been carried into effect, either because the

---

47. William Orme, *Memoirs of the Life, Writings and Religious Connexions of John Owen* (London: T. Hamilton, 1820), 101-2; and James Seaton Reid, *A History of the Presbyterian Church in Ireland*, 2nd ed (London: Whittaker and Co., 1853), 2:136. The latter is not the edition Miller cites, but it is the material referenced.

48. [S.M.] [John] Milton's work, entitled "A Treatise of Civil Power in Ecclesiastical Causes," was published in 1659. [John] Locke's first Letter on Toleration was published, in Holland, in the Latin language, in 1689.

magistrates have withheld their consent, or because the Church has never asked the necessary permission. The original manuscript of the "Acts of the Synod of Dort," having been put into the possession of the States General, they, in the year 1625, resolved that that manuscript should, *every three years*, be inspected by delegates from their own body, and deputies from the provincial Synods jointly. Accordingly this ceremony, we are told, is gone through, with a punctilious formality, in the month of May of every third year. Twenty-two deputies from the Synods repair to the Hague where they are joined by two delegates of the secular government. This joint body then proceeds to the public chamber in which the chest containing the Acts of the Synod are deposited. This chest is opened with eight several keys. The Acts, which are neatly bound up in seventeen volumes, are formally taken out and shown, first to the governmental delegates, and then to the clerical members of the body. This ceremony is preceded and followed with prayer, after which the members of the inspecting committee dine together, and thus terminates their triennial task.

The venerable Dr. Scott was prompted, he tells us, to undertake the translation of the official history and canons of the Synod of Dort, by the persuasion that they had been greatly misapprehended by the religious public, in which he had himself, for many years, largely participated. The truth is, the misrepresentations of the proceedings of that Synod by Peter Heylin, and Daniel Tilenus, are so gross and shameful, that it is difficult adequately to animadvert upon them in strictly temperate language.[49] As to Peter Heylin, he hardly knew how to speak the truth when Calvinism or Presbyterianism was in question. And, with respect to Daniel Tilenus, who was a theological Professor in the Presbyterian seminary at Sedan, in France, and had been once a Calvinist, but afterwards joined the Arminian ranks, his prejudices against his old opinions became, after his apostasy, so perfectly bitter and blinding, that he seemed incapable of representing them otherwise than under the most revolting caricature. No wonder that those who believed these men, regarded the Acts of the Synod with abhorrence. Dr. Scott, as the reader will perceive, declares himself satisfied, that the proceedings of the Synod had been greatly and criminally slandered; that their canons were

---

49. Peter Heylin (1599-1662) was an English Anglican author and historian. Daniel Tilenus (1563-1633) was a German-French Protestant theologian.

among the most Scriptural and excellent formularies he had ever seen; and that he thought it incumbent on him to do all in his power to remove the vail from the false statements concerning them which had been so confidently made, and to the circulation of which he had himself, in some degree, unintentionally contributed.

This translation was among the last works if not the very last, which Dr. Scott gave to the public. It was published only a few months prior to his decease, and was prepared by him under an immediate impression of that solemn account which he was so nearly approaching, and of the duty which be owed to the public in behalf of a greatly injured body.

The following remarks of Mons. Bayle, in his Biographical Dictionary, under the article Arminius, are so apposite and pointed as to form a very appropriate extract for this Introductory Essay.[50] Bayle himself was, probably, neither a Calvinist nor an Arminian, but a cool insidious sceptic. His judgment, therefore, on this controversy, may be considered as the decision of a shrewd, and, as to this point, an impartial mind, on a matter concerning which he had no point to gain, or party to serve.

"It were to be wished that he (Arminius) had made a better use of his knowledge. I mean, that he had governed himself by St. Paul's rule. This great Apostle, immediately inspired by God, and directed by the Holy Ghost in all his writings, raised to himself the objection which the light of nature forms against the doctrine of absolute predestination. He apprehended the whole force of the objection; and he proposes it without weakening it in the least degree. 'God hath mercy on whom he will have mercy, and whom he will he hardeneth' (Romans 9:18). This is Paul's doctrine; and the difficulty which he starts upon it is this – 'Thou wilt say, then, unto me, Why doth he yet find fault, for who hath resisted his will?' This objection cannot be pushed further; twenty pages, by the most subtle Molinist, could add nothing to it. What more could they infer than that, upon Calvin's hypothesis, God wills men to commit sin? Now this is what St. Paul knew might be objected against him; but what does he reply? Does he seek for distinctions and qualifications? Does he deny the fact? Does

---

50. Pierre Bayle (1647-1706) was a French Protestant philosopher, best known for his *Historical and Critical Dictionary* (1695-1697).

he grant it in part only? Does he enter into particulars? Does he remove any ambiguity in the words? Nothing of all this. He only alleges the sovereign power of God, and the supreme right which the Creator has to dispose of his creatures as it seems good to him. 'Nay, but O man, who art thou that repliest against God?' He acknowledges an incomprehensibility in the thing which ought to put a stop to all disputes, and to impose a profound silence on our reason. He cries out, 'O the depth of the riches both of the wisdom and knowledge of God! How unsearchable are his judgments, and his ways are past finding out.' All Christians ought to find here a definitive sentence, a judgment final, and without appeal in the dispute about grace. Or rather, they should learn from this conduct of St. Paul never to dispute about predestination, and immediately to oppose this bar against all the subtleties of human wit, whether they arise of themselves, in meditating on this great subject, or whether others suggest them. The best and the shortest way is, early to oppose this strong bank against the inundations of reasoning, and to consider this definitive sentence of St. Paul as a rock immoveable in the midst of the waves, against which the proudest billows may beat in vain. They may foam and dash, but are only broken against them. All arrows darted against this shield, will have the same fate as that of Priam."

Further on, the same writer says, "To a system full of great difficulties, Arminius has substituted another system, which, to speak truly, involves no less difficulties than the former. One may say of his doctrine what I have observed of the innovations of Saumur. It is better connected, and less forced than the opinions of Mr. Amyraut; but, after all, it is but a palliative remedy; for the Arminians have scarcely been able to answer some objections which, as they pretend, cannot be refuted upon Calvin's system. Besides, they find themselves exposed to other difficulties which they cannot get over but by an ingenuous confession of the weakness of human reason, and the consideration of the incomprehensible infinity of God. And was it worthwhile to contradict Calvin for this? Why was Arminius so very difficult at first, when, at last, he was obliged to fly to this asylum? Why did he not begin here, since here he must come sooner or later? He is mistaken who imagines that, after entering the lists with a great disputant, he shall be allowed to triumph only for some small advantage which he had over him at first. An athletic, who throws out his antagonist in the middle of the race, but has not the advantage of him at the end, is not entitled to the palm. It is the same in controversy. It is not sufficient to parry the first thrusts. Every reply and rejoinder must be satisfied, and every doubt perfectly cleared up. Now this is what neither the hypothesis of Arminius, nor that of the Molinists, nor that of the Socinians is able to do. The system of the Arminians is only calculated to give some few advantages in those preludes to war, in which the forlorn hope is sent out to skirmish. But when it comes to a general and decisive battle, this detachment must retire, as well as the rest, behind the entrenchments of incomprehensible mystery."[51]

Perhaps it may be said, that no theological system was ever more grossly misrepresented, or more foully or unjustly vilified than that which is commonly called Calvinism; but which had been drawn from the word of God, and preached by some of the best men that ever lived, many hundreds of years before Calvin was born. The truth is, it would be difficult to name a writer or speaker who has distinguished himself by opposing this system, who has fairly represented it, or who really appeared to understand it. They are forever fighting against an imaginary monster of their own creation. They picture to themselves the consequences which they suppose unavoidably flow from the real principles of Calvinists, and then, most unjustly, represent these consequences as a part of the system itself, as held by its advocates. Whether this arises from the want of knowledge, or the want of candor, is not for me to decide; but the effect is the same, and the conduct worthy of severe censure. How many an eloquent page of anti-Calvinistic declamation would be instantly seen by every reader to be either calumny or nonsense, if it had been preceded by an honest statement of what the system, as held by Calvinists, really is!

The enemies of the system allege, that it represents God as really the author of sin, and man as laid under a physical necessity of sinning, and then as damned for it, do what he can. They insist that our doctrine of *depravity*, and the mode of inheriting it, if true, destroys moral agency; reduces men to the condition of mere machines; and, of course, makes all punishment of sin unjust and absurd. In short, they contend, that the views which we give of the plan of salvation, makes

---

51. Peter Bayle, *An Historical and Critical Dictionary*, 4 vol. (London: Hunt and Clarke, 1826), 1:158-62.

a system of heathenish fate, or of refined Antinomianism, equally destructive of holiness and of comfort; and that, under the guise of free grace, we build up a fabric of favoritism on the one hand, and of fixed necessity on the other; at once making God a partial being, and a tyrant, and man a mere passive subject of his arbitrary will. But, is it true that Calvinists embrace any such system as this? Nothing can be further from the truth. It is a shameful misrepresentation, which has no correspondence with anything but the caricatures of prejudice and bigotry. Calvinists abhor such sentiments just as much as their uncandid accusers. Many wise and excellent men have been of the opinion that Arminian principles, when traced out to their natural and unavoidable consequences, lead to an invasion of the essential attributes of God, and, of course, to blank and cheerless atheism. Yet, in making a statement of the Arminian system, as actually held by its advocates, what candid man would allow himself to introduce into the delineation anything different from or beyond the actual admissions of those advocates? The system itself is one thing; the consequences which may be drawn from it another.

It is not pretended that the Calvinistic system is free from all difficulties. When finite creatures are called to scan either the works or the revealed will of an Infinite Being, they must be truly demented if they expect to find nothing which is incomprehensible. Accordingly, when we undertake to solve some of the difficulties which the Calvinistic system presents, it cannot be denied that "such knowledge is too wonderful for us; it is high, we cannot attain unto it." How to reconcile what the Scriptures plainly reveal, on the one hand, concerning the entire dependence of man; and, on the other, concerning his activity and responsibility; how to explain the perfect foreknowledge and predestination of God, in consistency with the perfect freedom and moral agency of his intelligent creatures, is a problem which no thinking man expects fully to solve. But the question is, are there fewer difficulties attending any other system? Especially are there fewer difficulties attending the Arminian or Pelagian system, one or the other of which is usually the resort of those who reject Calvinism? There are not; nay, instead of being less, they are greater – far greater both in number and magnitude. For example, it is easy, and, in the estimation of the superficial and unreflecting, it appears conclusive, to object, that Calvinism has a tendency to cut the nerves of all Spiritual exertion; that if we are elected, we shall be saved, do what we will; and, if not elected, we shall be lost, do what we can. But is it not perfectly evident, that the objection here lies with quite as much force against the Arminian or Pelagian hypothesis? Arminians and Pelagians both grant that all men will not actually be saved; that the salvation or perdition of each individual is distinctly foreknown by God; and that the event will certainly happen as He foresees that it will. May not a caviler, then, say, with quite as much appearance of justice, in this case, as in the other; "the result, as to my salvation, though unknown to me, is known to God, and certain. If I am to be saved, no anxiety about it is necessary; and if I am to perish, all anxiety about it would be useless." But would an Arminian consider such an objection as valid against his creed? Probably not. Yet it is certainly just as valid against his creed as against ours. The truth is, the Arminian, by resorting to his scheme, does not really get rid of one particle of the difficulty which he alleges against the Calvinistic system: he only places it one step further back, but must meet it in its full strength after all. Until we can bring ourselves to swallow the monstrous absurdity, that what is to be, will not be; that what God foresees as certain, may never happen, the cavil, such as it is, remains unanswered. If there be a God who is endowed with perfect foreknowledge, and who is, and always has been, acting upon a plan, of which he knows the end from the beginning – and there is such a Being, or there is no God – then all the difficulty which lies against the doctrine of sovereign, unconditional predetermination, lies equally, and in all its unmitigated force, against the doctrine of foreknowledge and certain futurition, in any form that can be imagined; and all the shocking consequences with which they charge Calvinism, are quite as legitimately chargeable against any and every scheme, short of Atheism, which may be embraced to get rid of them.

No other proof of this is needed than the subterfuges to which Arminians and Pelagians have resorted in order to obviate the objections which they have felt pressing on their respective schemes. Some have denied the possibility of God's foreknowing future contingencies; alleging that such foreknowledge cannot be conceived or admitted, more than the power of doing impossibilities, or doing what involves a contradiction. Others have denied the plenary foreknowledge of God altogether; alleging that there are many things which he does not choose to know – the latter making the divine ignorance of many future things voluntary, while the former consider it as necessary. A third class, to get rid of the same difficulties, take refuge in the principle that the Most High is deficient in power as well as in knowledge; that his plan – so far as he has any – is continually thwarted and opposed beyond his power of control. That he would be glad to have less natural and moral evil in his kingdom than exists; would be glad to have many more saved than will be saved; but is not able to fulfil his wishes; and is constantly restrained and defeated by his own creatures!

Do not these boasted refuges from Calvinism shock every mind not thoroughly hardened and profane? Do not the allegations that God is not omnipotent; that he is not omniscient; that he is not acting upon an eternal and settled plan; that his purposes, instead of being eternal, are all formed in time; and instead of being immutable, are all liable to be altered every day, and are, in fact, altered by the changing will of his creatures; that there is no certainty of his predictions and promises ever being fulfilled, because he can neither foresee nor control future contingencies; that it is his express design to save all men alike, while yet it is certain that all will not be saved; that he purposes as much, and does as much for those who perish, as for those who are saved; but is, after all, baffled and disappointed in his hopes concerning them; that he is certain of nothing, because he has determined on nothing, positively, and, if he had, is not able to do all his pleasure – do not such allegations fill every thinking mind with horror? Are they not equally contrary to Scripture, to reason, and to all the hopes and consolations of the pious? Would not such a God, with reverence be it spoken, be the most unhappy being in the universe? True, indeed, Arminians do not recognize these horrid consequences, and, therefore, cannot be charged with holding them; but they are not, on this account, the less inevitable, or the less awful.

But though that system of grace usually denominated Calvinism, is now in such bad odor with multitudes in the Church of England, and with many connected with her ecclesiastical Daughter in this country – it was not always so. When the Synod of Dort convened, the same theological system which that celebrated Synod sustained, was the reigning creed in the Church of England, and had been so, beyond all question, for more than half a century. This has, indeed, been denied; but it would be just as reasonable to deny that such men as Cranmer and Whitgift, and Hooker, and Hall, and Usher ever occupied stations in the established Church of that land. Testimony to establish the position which has been assumed, which prejudice itself cannot refute, crowds upon us, and offers itself on every side.

The testimony of Peter Heylin, a bitter enemy to Calvinism, is clear and decisive. "It cannot be denied," says he, "but that, by the error of these times, the reputation which Calvin had attained to in both Universities, and the extreme diligence of his followers, there was a general tendency unto his opinions; his book of Institutes being, for the most part, the foundation on which the young divines of those days did build their studies." Again he declares – "Of any men who publicly opposed the Calvinian tenets, in the university of Oxford, till after the beginning of King James's reign, I must confess that I have hitherto found no good assurance." He speaks of two divines of inferior note, who secretly propagated Arminian principles; and compares them to the prophet Elijah, who considered himself as left alone to oppose a whole world of idolaters. Further: in the reign of Charles I, more than sixty years after the final settling of the thirty-nine Articles, when a suppression of the Calvinistic doctrines was contemplated by Archbishop Laud, Heylin acknowledges that such was the general attachment of the bishops and clergy to these doctrines, that the Arminian party did not dare to "venture the determining of these points to a Convocation." And he again explicitly informs us, that, from the re-settling of the Church under Queen Elizabeth, to the period already mentioned, "the maintainers of the anti-Calvinian doctrines were few in number, and made but a very thin appearance."[52]

The famous Lambeth Articles, drawn up in 1595, during the reign of Queen Elizabeth, are acknowledged by all who ever read them, to be among the most strongly marked Calvinistical compositions that ever were penned. They were drawn up by Archbishop Whitgift, then at the head of the English established Church, and one of its most conspicuous divines and fathers. The archbishop was assisted in this service by the bishops of London and Bangor, and by some others. After receiving the public approbation of these dignitaries, the Articles were sent to the Archbishop of York, and the Bishop of Rochester, who also

---

52. [S.M.] See Heylin's Quinq. Hist. Work, p. 626, etc. See also his Life of Laud, p. 147. [Peter Heylyn, *The Historical and Miscellaneous Tracts of Peter Heylyn* (London, 1681), 626-27; and Heylyn, *Cyprianus Anglicus: or, the History of the Life and Death, of the most Rev. William, Lord Archbishop of Canterbury* (London, 1668), 147.]

subscribed them. Thus ratified, Archbishop Whitgift sent them to the University of Cambridge, with a letter, in which he declared – "That these Articles were not to be considered as laws and decrees, but as propositions, which he and his brethren were persuaded were true, and corresponding with the doctrine professed in the Church of England, and established by the laws of the land." Nor is this all: it having been suggested by some, that the Archbishop agreed to these Articles rather for the sake of peace, than because he believed them, Strype, his Episcopal biographer, repels the charge with indignation, declaring that such an insinuation is as false as it is mean and disparaging to the primate.[53]

Not long after the delegates to the Synod of Dort, from the Church of England, returned home, they were attacked by certain writers, who reproached them for having signed the Articles of the Synod, and charged them with having, by that act, given countenance to error, and also with having departed from the Articles of their own Church. Against this attack they thought proper to defend themselves, by what they called a joint attestation, which contains the following passage: "Whatsoever there was assented unto, and subscribed by us, concerning the five Articles, either in the joint Synodical judgment, or in our particular collegiate suffrage, is not only warrantable by the holy Scriptures, but also conformable to the received doctrine of our said venerable mother, which we are ready to maintain and justify against all gainsayers."

Again, Bishop Hall, before mentioned as one of the delegates, in a work of his own, addressed to some who had charged him, and some other bishops of his day, with entertaining Arminian sentiments as to the doctrine of election, thus indignantly replies to the charge: "You add, 'election upon faith foreseen.' What! nothing but gross untruths? Is this the doctrine of the bishops of England? Have they not strongly confuted it, in Papists and Arminians? Have they not cried it down to the lowest pit of hell?"[54]

---

53. [S.M.] Strype's Life of Whitgift, p. 461-463. [John Strype, *The Life and Acts of John Whitgift* (Oxford: Clarendon Press, 1822), 460-68. Strype (1643-1737) was an English Anglican clergyman and historian.]

54. [S.M.] Defence of the Humble Remonstrance. Works, vol. iii, p. 246. [It is not apparent which edition of Hall's works Miller was using, but the quotation can be found in a 19th century edition of Hall's works here: *Joseph Hall, The Works of Joseph Hall: Volume X: Polemical Works* (Oxford: D.A. Talboys, 1837), 349. The original publication was: *Joseph Hall, A Defence of the Humble Remonstrance* (London, 1641), 153-54.]

The same pious prelate himself tells us, that after his return from the Synod of Dort, where he had been, as we have seen, an advocate of Calvinistic doctrine, and a warm and open opponent of Arminianism, he was distressed to find that heresy gaining ground in England. "Not many years," says he, "after settling at home, it grieved my soul to see our own Church begin to sicken of the same disease, which we had endeavored to cure in our neighbors."[55]

That the thirty-nine Articles of the Church of England are Calvinistic, has been so often asserted and demonstrated, that a new attempt to establish the fact is certainly unnecessary. The seventeenth Article in particular bears ample testimony to this fact. I am aware, indeed, that it has been alleged, that the qualifying clause, toward the end of the Article, shows that the framers of it meant to reject Calvinism. Now it so happens that the very qualifying clause in question, is nearly copied from Calvin's Institutes, and the latter part of that clause is a literal translation of that Reformer's caution against the abuse of this doctrine. For evidence of the former, see his Institutes III.21.4-5, compared with the Article, where every idea contained in that part of the Article will be found recited. For proof of the latter, read the following: "Proinde, in rebus agendis, ea est nobis perspicienda Dei voluntas quam verbo suo declarat." Instit. I.17.5.[56] "Furthermore, in our doings, that will of God is to be followed, which we have expressly declared to us in the word of God." Art. 17th.[57]

A correspondent of the Christian Observer, a clergyman of the established Church of England, in speaking of the disposition of many in his own church, to vilify the name and opinions of Calvin, makes the following remarks:

"Few names stand higher, or in more deserved pre-eminence, among the

---

55. [S.M.] Some Specialties of the Life of Joseph Hall, Bishop of Norwich, written by himself, prefixed to the third volume of his works. [This quotation can be found here: Joseph Hall, *The Works of the Right Reverend Father in God, Joseph Hall: Volume 1: Contemplations* (London: C. Whittingham, 1808), xli.]

56. "So then, in the things to be conducted, it is for us to examine the will of God which he declares by his Word." Special thanks to Dr. Harrison Perkins for the English translation of Calvin's quotation.

57. [S.M.] For this reference, to show that the 17th Article is not to be interpreted as opposed to Calvinism, see *Christian Observer, of London*, vol. iii. p. 438. [Review of Charles Daubeny, *Vindiciæ Ecclesiæ Anglicanæ*, in *The Christian Observer* Vol. 3, No. 7 (July 1804): 425-39.]

wise and pious members of the English Church, than that of Bishop Andrews. His testimony to the memory of Calvin is, that he was, an illustrious person, and never to be mentioned without a preface of the highest honor. Whoever examines into the sermons, writings, etc. of our divines in the reign of Elizabeth, and James I, will continually meet with epithets of honor with which his name is mentioned; the learned, the wise, the judicious, the pious Calvin, are expressions everywhere to be found in the remains of those times. It is well known that his Institutes were read and studied in the universities, by every student in divinity; nay, that, by a convocation held at Oxford, that book was recommended to the general study of the nation. So far was the Church of England, and her chief divines, from countenancing that unbecoming and absurd treatment with which the name of this eminent Protestant is now so frequently dishonored, that it would be no difficult matter to prove, that there is not, perhaps, a parallel instance upon record, of any single individual being equally, and so unequivocally venerated, for the union of wisdom and piety, both in England and by a large body of the foreign churches, as John Calvin. Nothing but ignorance of the ecclesiastical records of those times, or resolute prejudice, could cast a cloak of concealment over this fact. It has been evidenced by the combined testimony both of enemies and friends to his system of doctrines."[58]

---

58. [S.M.] Christian Observer, vol. ii, p. 143. [Anonymous "Curate from the South," "Opinion Entertained of Calvin by Our First Reformers," in *The Christian Observer* Vol. 2, No. 3 (March 1803): 143-144.]

Other Publications
By Log College Press

The Duties of a Gospel Minister

John Holt Rice

Aging In Grace
Letters to Those in the Autumn of Life

Archibald Alexander

Christ All in All
The Right Temper for a Theologian

William Swan Plumer

The Five Points of Presbyterianism

The Distinctives of Presbyterian Church Government

Thomas Dwight Witherspoon

A Forty-Three Year Pastorate in a Country Church

C. W. Grafton

MEDITATIONS
ON PREACHING

Francis James Grimké